PRESCHOOL

AND

EARLY ELEMENTARY ART BASICS

By

Rich and Sharon Jeffus

This book is dedicated to my mother, Elinor Brewer.
Thanks to her for all her help and encouragement!
Proverbs 22:6 *Train up a child in the way he should go: and when he is old, he will not depart from it.*

TABLE OF CONTENTS

Introduction

My purpose in writing this book is to provide preschool and younger children a simple beginning in art education. It really is as easy as 1, 2, 3! A young child can easily learn all about art by learning art appreciation, basic shapes, color and creativity. I have found some secrets about doing art with younger children from working with hundreds of them on a daily basis. When we do our art lessons, we move very quickly. Each project incorporates simple vocabulary of the arts, art appreciation, and making a project together using basic shapes. Vocabulary will be in bold letters. Young children, I believe, benefit by a variety of media while doing their projects. I keep not only oil pastels, (you could use crayons) and markers, but also scissors, glue and scrap paper. I also purchase sparkles or other smaller items they can glue on their paper. You can even use a hole punch and have dots for them to glue on. This develops fine motor skills. When I draw with preschool/kindergarten children, I draw one line at a time. This way they are not overwhelmed. Keep things simple. Encouraging creativity is very important. Kind words mean so very much. When we do our lessons on appreciation, I have included some details for older students or moms! I have found when students do a simple project after looking at a master work of art....they can remember more about the work of art. **I have listed websites which display the pictures on a larger scale. These pictures can be printed out from the computer with a color printer.**

Preschool Art Characteristics

In most children ages 2-4, the child uses all of his senses when working with the material. When we do workshops with little ones, we use scented markers instead of regular markers, and a wide variety of sensory materials for them to manipulate. The child will make marks on their paper attempting to control their crayon or marker. Children between 2 and 4 love to work with clay. It is an important event when they begin to name their creations. I believe much benefit can be gained from showing children of this age master works of art. It is important to mention the vocabulary of the arts when mentioning the works of art. As the attention span is short, you must limit this presentation to only 2 or three minutes, and then repeat it several times during the project. The same is true of children in the early symbolic stage.

The early symbolic age in art is approximately 4-7. The child creates symbols for the things he wants to communicate using lines and shapes. In most cases, children put on the paper only the most important part of what they are communicating. As the teacher, you must be sure to use as many vocabulary words as possible, naming the lines and shapes several times. Make sure that when you do a picture of a person with them, that you call it a portrait. Maybe the lady will just be a circle and hair, eyes and a smile. When you tell them, "Where is the nose?" they smile and say they forgot the nose! Don't worry about what the finished product looks like. They need to feel good about what they are creating and communicating. I believe coloring books are not good at this stage of development. It is better for them to draw their own creations and color them in to develop fine motor skills. In the later symbolic stage ages 5-9, the child doesn't worry about what he sees, but just does symbolic pictures of his feelings and thoughts. He can be taught to put in horizon line, clouds, foreground, background and a wide variety of other art forms. For one of the best explanations of children's art at the preschool level, I recommend Art for the Fun of It, by Peggy Davison Jenkins. At a certain point, the child will want to know how to get their pictures to look real. Then you can step in and teach shading, shadow and texture. That is in another book.

THE **CENTER OF INTEREST** IS WHAT CATCHES YOUR EYE FIRST IN A WORK OF ART.

The Jolly Flatboatmen
by George Caleb Bingham
Over 100 years ago, before telephones, ice cream, and automobiles, George Caleb Bingham was doing wonderful pictures of life on the Missouri and Mississippi Rivers. When Mark Twain was writing about Tom Sawyer and Huckleberry Finn, Bingham was picturing the river life in drawings and paintings. Go to this web site to see the picture in color and enjoy a wonderful free art lesson on the way Bingham put his compositions together. <http://www.slam.org/flatboat.html>.
Here is a part of an article written from the *Bingham Times* available at the St. Louis Art Museum. “One day I was messing around on my raft, kind of dancing around. This fellow came along and stood on the bank staring at me....He had painted a picture of me on my raft. It was beautiful...He told me he was a painter. He paid me fifty cents for using me in his work. Said his name was Bingham...All the kids made fun of me because I was poor and wore the same clothes to school all the time. They teased me because I always tied a red kerchief around my collar.....I loved playing in the river. I liked building rafts, floating on the water like I was Huck Finn.....I’m grown now. My friends come and play music while I dance on my raft. I’m really jolly.” This is just part of how the painting might have come about. The center of interest is the red kerchief being held up in the air. Because it is red, it attracts your attention first. Although the picture in this book is black and white, you can color the scarf red and see what a center of interest is.

The Jolly Flatboatmen, 1857, by George Caleb Bingham Courtesy of the St. Louis Art Museum

The County Election, 1851 - 1852
by George Caleb Bingham
Courtesy of the St. Louis Art Museum Purchase

Here is another delightful picture done by George Caleb Bingham. We are just passing by this scene and get a glimpse of what life is like at a county election along the Missouri River in the 1880's. Before people were doing photography, artists pictured what life was like. Look at the clothing in this picture. Notice the boys playing in the front (foreground) of the picture. Nearly everyone is busy talking to other people. They are probably discussing the election. There is no formal posing in this picture. We are just watching a scene from everyday life. What do you look at first in this picture?

Raftsmen Playing Cards, 1847
by George Caleb Bingham
Saint Louis Art Museum. Ezra H. Linley Fund.

George Caleb Bingham was born in 1811 in Virginia. He emigrated to Missouri at the age of 21 and became a portrait painter along the Missouri and Mississippi Rivers. He did over 1000 portraits of everyday people. These men are not dressed fancy. Some are barefoot. But they exude a confident and independent feeling. Does it help you to understand what people were like in the middle of the 17th century on the Missouri and Mississippi Rivers? George Caleb Bingham is even honored by the American people so much, that he has a painting in the White House.

Follow these easy directions to make a riverboat. At the same time Mark Twain was writing about life on the Mississippi River, Bingham was doing river pictures. Make your water first. You can use torn blue paper and paste your water on your paper. You can use blue crayons, oil pastels, markers or paints. I have children draw with markers or oil pastels. I only give them a pencil when they request one.

1

Mona Lisa

by
Leonardo da Vinci
1452-1519

THE **CENTER OF INTEREST** IS THE LADY!

Look at the pretty lady. Her name is Mona Lisa. She lived over 500 years ago. Mona Lisa is one of the most famous pictures in the world. Although it is small in size, it is great in the wonderful way it was painted (**technique**). Leonardo did this painting around the age of 50. It is said that he painted the wife of an Italian nobleman who had recently lost a child. She was very sad because of this, and Leonardo hired musicians to play while he painted her. He obviously wanted her smiling and just caught that ever so lightly hint of a smile to be recorded for history. Have you ever tried to make someone smile and finally, they gave you just a hint of a smile? Some people say that her hands were the most beautifully painted in history.

Leonardo da Vinci liked to invent different things. Art is taking things that are different and putting them together to make your own original picture. Can you draw a lady? Look at the example. Can you make details on the picture? Count the number of things you can draw on the great lady's face. Put eyelashes on the eyes. Can you think of more details to put in the picture?

A **PORTRAIT** IS A REALISTIC PICTURE OF A PERSON!

More About Leonardo da Vinci

Leonardo da Vinci was very famous as one of the great master artists of all time. He lived from 1452-1519. He was interested in many facets of art and invention. He loved to draw things from nature. When he was very young, his father discovered he had quite a talent for art. He looked at frogs and lizards from nature and came up with a dragon for a shield that scared his own father. Maybe you like to draw dinosaurs? Maybe you will be as famous as Leonardo some day. At 15 years of age, Leonardo was apprenticed (went to live with and learn from) a great painter and sculptor from France, Verrocchio. In his 20's, Leonardo had a studio of his own. He did wonderful work showing shading, shadow and texture in his art. Leonardo left Florence to go to Milan. He did what was close to his heart. His job was titled "Painter and Engineer to the Duke," He not only painted portraits, he did sets and costumes for theatre, and gave advice on military architecture and even mechanical engineering. His use of light and shadow (chiaroscuro) made his figures look rounded. Leonardo designed weapons and flying machines, and a submarine. How marvelous are his inventions. He had a problem of many times working slowly or not finishing a project. This was the case with his magnificent horse, the Statue of Francesco Sforza. An amazing thing about Leonardo da Vinci was the way in which he excelled at all of the arts. He was a writer, a poet, a sculptor, an accomplished musician, and a painter.

The Arts Reflect Each Other
The highest authorities consider all the arts as one in fundamental principles, if not in aim. Phidias, Giotto, Leonardo da Vinci, Michelangelo, and the greatest artists of all time, were not specialists in one art, but students of every form of art. They were painters, architects, sculptors, musicians and poets. The arts reflect each other; the terms which are applied to the arts are borrowed from each other. We speak of a picture, and the color of a piece of music. The sculptor must have a sense of color and music, or his work will be cold. Each art may definitely require a special set of faculties to be trained, but these are co-relative and must be brought into harmony for power in any one art. Hence a certain amount of training in different arts develops the art capacities, and enables the mind to grasp the elements that are fundamental to all art. S. S. Curry

Sfumato is the term used for the background in the "Mona Lisa." Look at the hazy background. Look at the trees and water in the distance. It is slightly blurred. Mona Lisa is in the **foreground**, or front of the picture. The landscape is in the **background**, or back of the picture. The **horizon line** is the place where the sky and the land meet. Notice how the sky is slightly lighter on the horizon line in the background. It gets darker as you go to the top of the sky. You can put this in your pictures, too.

For a large print of the Mona Lisa you can print out go to <http://www.artchive.com/artchive/L/leonardo/monalisa.jpg.html>.

1 Rabbit

A Young Hare, 1502
by Albecht Durer

Did you know that a hare and a rabbit are the same thing? This is one rabbit. It is by a Renaissance artist named Durer. He did wonderful pictures with many details. The artist used many lines to get the fur to look like fur. In art, this is called **implied texture**. This rabbit is brown. Brown is not on the color wheel. Brown is a neutral color. Can you draw a rabbit? Can you color it brown? Use basic shapes to make a rabbit. Will your rabbit be in the forest? Will it be in the grass? Look at the rabbit below. I started with a small circle and a large circle. I made two C's that were backward for the leg. I put on a circle for a tail and two long ovals for ears. Just add a nose and an eye and he is a rabbit!

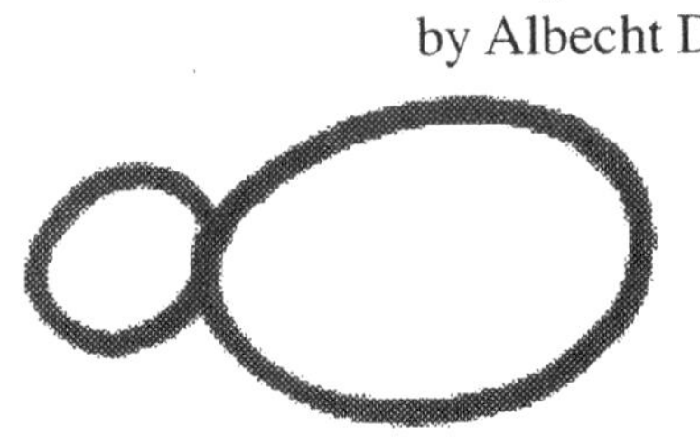

A friend of mine wrote a story about a rabbit named Snowball. Do you know how Dumbo was an elephant with very large ears? Snowball was a rabbit with very large ears, too. He had a frog who loved him just as he was....just like Jesus loves us. My friend asked me to create what Snowball looked like. You can do what I do and create a cartoon rabbit, too.

WHAT IS THE **CENTER OF INTEREST?** THE RABBIT, OF COURSE!

"I hold that the perfection of form and beauty is contained in the sum of all men." Four Books on Human Proportions, 1528.

Albrecht Durer was from Nuremburg, Germany. According to Janson's History of Art he was the leading printmaker of his time. He has a wide influence on all European art through his woodcuts and engravings which circulated throughout all of Europe. He did amazing pictures of Biblical themes. His "Four Horsemen of the Apocalypse" influenced great change in the art of woodcuts. According to Janson's History of Art, "In his hands, woodcuts lose their former charm as popular art, but gain the precise articulation of a fully matured graphic style." In later years, Durer wrote a paper on geometry based on a study of perspective. He invented a device for producing an image by mechanical means...in essence this was the first step in the development of the photographic camera.

It is said that Albecht Durer had a brother who worked very hard so that he could be an artist. We will also read about another artist in this book named Van Gogh who had a brother who loved him and supported him so he could paint. It is said that Durer loved his brother so much that he did this picture of his hands. These have become very famous, appearing in paintings and sculptures. I collect pictures and statues of praying hands. My husband, who is a sculptor, sculpted praying hands. A drawing is a one dimensional piece of art. He did a drawing of the praying hands first. Then he sculpted them making a three dimensional art work of art.. If you had a brother or sister who wanted to be an artist, would you get a job so you could support them so they could paint? Durer and Van Gogh can both thank their brother.

Go to this web site to see a wonderful picture of the praying hands:<http://sunsite.dk/cgfa/durer/p-durer48.htm>.

One of the easiest ways to print with younger children is to take a foam meat tray that is cleaned and dry and use a pencil to carve a design in the tray. I allow them to use dauber paint to go over the marks they have made. Then they press it on to a paper. Any of the drawing lessons in this book would work well for a meat tray design.

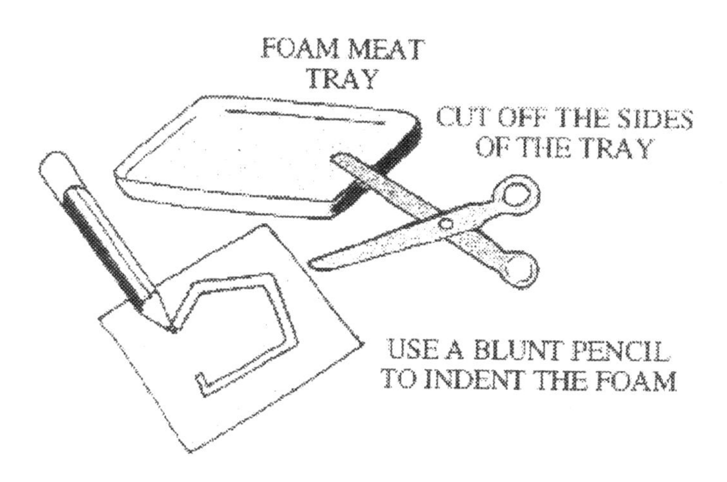

2 KINDS OF
SPACE
POSITIVE/
NEGATIVE

2 Kinds of Space

When I teach **positive/negative space**, I always use Rembrandt as an example. This is his self-portrait. It is believed he did over 60 of these. Rembrandt is considered the greatest genius of Dutch art and perhaps the master of the Baroque movement in art. He did many wonderful pictures from the Old Testament. He brought scenes from the Bible to life. He was a master at using the contrast of light (positive space), and dark (negative space). I love to do the lighthouse picture below with little children. Look on the following page for instructions in drawing a lighthouse scene. It is important to have one side of the paper black. You can explain about using light color crayon on dark paper to achieve **contrast.** I encourage students to draw a tall ship in the picture (see lesson on tall ship). We have wonderful conversations about life around the lighthouse.

Self-portrait by Rembrandt

A light house is a very simple thing to draw with young children. It is composed of just a few lines. The fun comes in thinking of things to add to your picture. How about a full moon in the night picture? Of course, the word nocturnal needs to be explained. You can talk about the sea turtles that lay their eggs at night on the beach, or the sea gulls that fly in the day!

Here are some great ideas to do with little children when learning positive/negative space and looking at art work by Rembrandt.

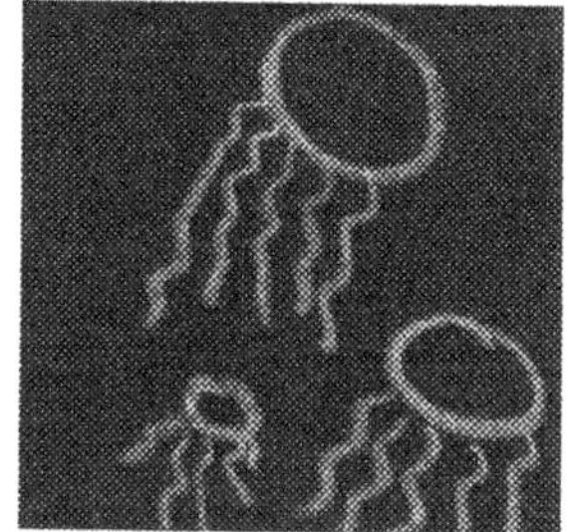

One of my favorite projects to do with children is making a jellyfish picture. I give them a black half sheet of paper and have them make jellyfish. I then pass out red paper for a border for their picture. We talk about pattern and put a jellyfish pattern on the border.

To see a self portrait of Rembrandt, go to : <http://sunsite.dk/cgfa/rembrand/p-rembra22.htm>. Rembrandt was a master printmaker, doing many wonderful **etchings**. An etching is done by making a drawing on metal or glass by the action of an acid, which eats into the areas laid bare by a special needle.

Another fun project to do with little children is to do an outer space picture. The black is negative space, the planets are positive space. Another great idea is a nocturnal picture. You can put owls, lightening bugs, etc. in your picture.

Do you like this picture? Is this a place you would like to go? The dark is negative space, the light is positive space.

3 KINDS
OF LINES
VERTICAL
HORIZONTAL
DIAGONAL

There are 3 kinds of lines. A **vertical** line looks like it is standing up straight. A **horizontal** line looks like it could be sleeping. A **diagonal** line looks like it is falling over. Many wonderful things can be made from horizontal, vertical and diagonal lines.

How many kinds of lines do you see in the number 3 on the left?

VERTICAL HORIZONTAL DIAGONAL

Look on the left and name each line you see.

TALL SHIP

Make a seascape out of vertical lines. I suggest making your water first out of blue torn paper. We use at least 2 shades of blue. To make a tall ship, you need to use horizontal, vertical and diagonal lines. You start with a base for your ship. You make 2 horizontal and 2 diagonal lines to do this. You make 3 vertical lines on your base. On each of the vertical lines, make 3 squares. On the top of the middle square, I put a triangle for a flag. Look at the next page for another lesson on drawing a tall ship.

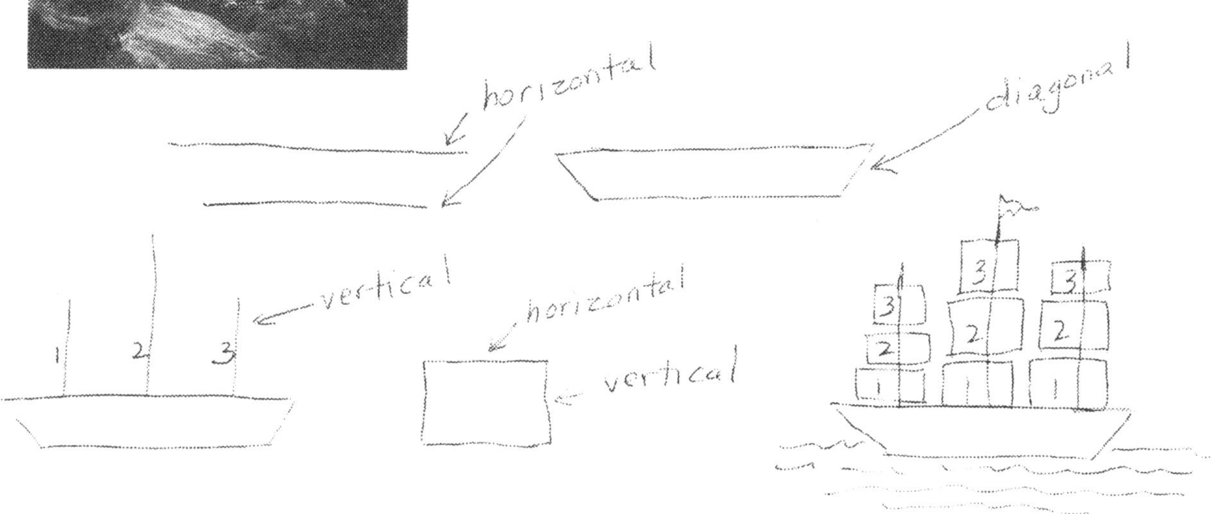

Gabe Stant age 6 Great job!

A **SEASCAPE** IS PRIMARILY A PICTURE OF THE LAND AND THE SEA.

Here are two kinds of boats made with horizontal and vertical lines. Practice making these boats.

3

Here are different ways to make a horse from **horizontal, vertical** and **diagonal** lines. Put a ground (horizon line) on your paper and make 3 horses. A horizon line is the place where the land and the sky meet. Can you see the horizon line outside of your window? Does a horse float in the air like a balloon? No, you need to put a horse on the **horizon line**.

How many babies are on the right?

Frederic Remington, *Harper's Weekly* October 1888

Do you like the cowboys? Have you ever pretended to be a cowboy or Indian? Much of the clothing you can buy to dress up western in was taken from pictures by Frederic Remington. Before the camera was used to picture the news, artists drew pictures of the happenings of the old west. Remington did many of these pictures. He loved horses and was most famous for drawing the horses and scenes of the west. He even had a door just for horses in his studio (the place where he did his art). Can you count 3 horses on the previous page? Notice how the horse in the **background** is the smallest. Notice how the horse in the **foreground** (front) is very large. Things in the foreground are larger. Things in the background are smaller.

More on Remington

"I knew the wild riders and the vacant land were about to vanish forever...and the more I considered the subject, the bigger the forever loomed. Without knowing how to do it, I began to record some facts around me, and the more I looked the more the panorama unfolded."

Everyone loves the American cowboys and Indians. When we are young, we pretend to be either a good cowboy, an outlaw, a lawman, an Indian, or a beautiful Indian princess. The choices are wonderful and endless. There is a famous American artist who helps us use our imagination when wondering what life in the wild west was really like. His name is Frederic Remington.

He only lived 48 years, but gave the world 2,739 pictures and 25 bronze sculptures. When he was only 16 years old he entered Yale as one of only two art students in the class. When his father died and left him a modest inheritance, he quit school and headed west in search of adventure. He probably had the same spirit of adventure to head west that so many pioneers had. After several years went by, of recording pictures of life in the west, he settled in New York and could name Teddy Roosevelt, and Rudyard Kipling as companions. There is a wonderful story about Remington. The publisher Hearst sent him to Cuba to cover the Spanish American War as an artist/correspondent. Remington reportedly complained to him that there wasn't any war. Hearst cabled him the famous comment
" You furnish the pictures, I'll furnish the war." Remington loved horses! His studio was built with barn doors so he could bring the horses in. He pictured every horse with its own personality....totally unique. He painted some horses galloping with all four hooves off the ground. He brought the horse to life for people who might never get to ride or see one in the old west. Teddy Roosevelt said of him,"He has portrayed a most characteristic and yet vanishing type of American life." He did many pictures mostly for Harper's Weekly in the late 1800's. Go to <http://www.artcyclopedia.com/artists/remington_frederic.html> He asked that on his tombstone would be the words, "He knew the Horse."

A Starry Night
by
Vincent Van Gogh

To see this picture enlarged in color go to:<http://www.moma.org/docs/collection/paintsculpt/c58.htm>.

SWIRLY LINES There are other kinds of lines. Look at the swirly lines above in this picture. This picture is called "Starry Night." Have you ever looked into a starry sky? Does it look like the stars are moving sometimes? Vincent Van Gogh did this picture in blues and yellows. Does it look like the lights are on in the houses? Get black paper and do a night picture. Can you make your stars look swirly?
Make a simple house shape. What do you think the black shape in the front of the picture is? Do you think it is a tree? You will learn how to make many different kinds of trees in Lesson 5. Can you make a tree in the foreground? Use one of your lessons on making the tree. Will you make a Y tree? Will you make a triangle tree? Will you make a torn

More on Vincent Van Gogh

Vincent Van Gogh has an interesting history. He was a great force in post Impressionism art. He is in a class in the art world that is all his own. He was going to go into the ministry, but in 1879, his career in the ministry ended. His brother, Theo, an artist who was living in Paris decided he would finance his brother while he painted. His brother must have loved him and believed in his painting. Van Gogh traveled to Paris where he was friends with Seurat, Gauguin, Pissaro, and Toulouse-Lautrec. He loved to use pure colors. It was very sad that he was committed to an asylum and seemed very unhappy most of his life. He painted glorious paintings for us to enjoy. He has a very unusual style. It is almost as if he does his whole painting in lines of paint. You can try this by doing a picture and coloring it in with lines instead of solid colors. Van Gogh used heavy brushstrokes.

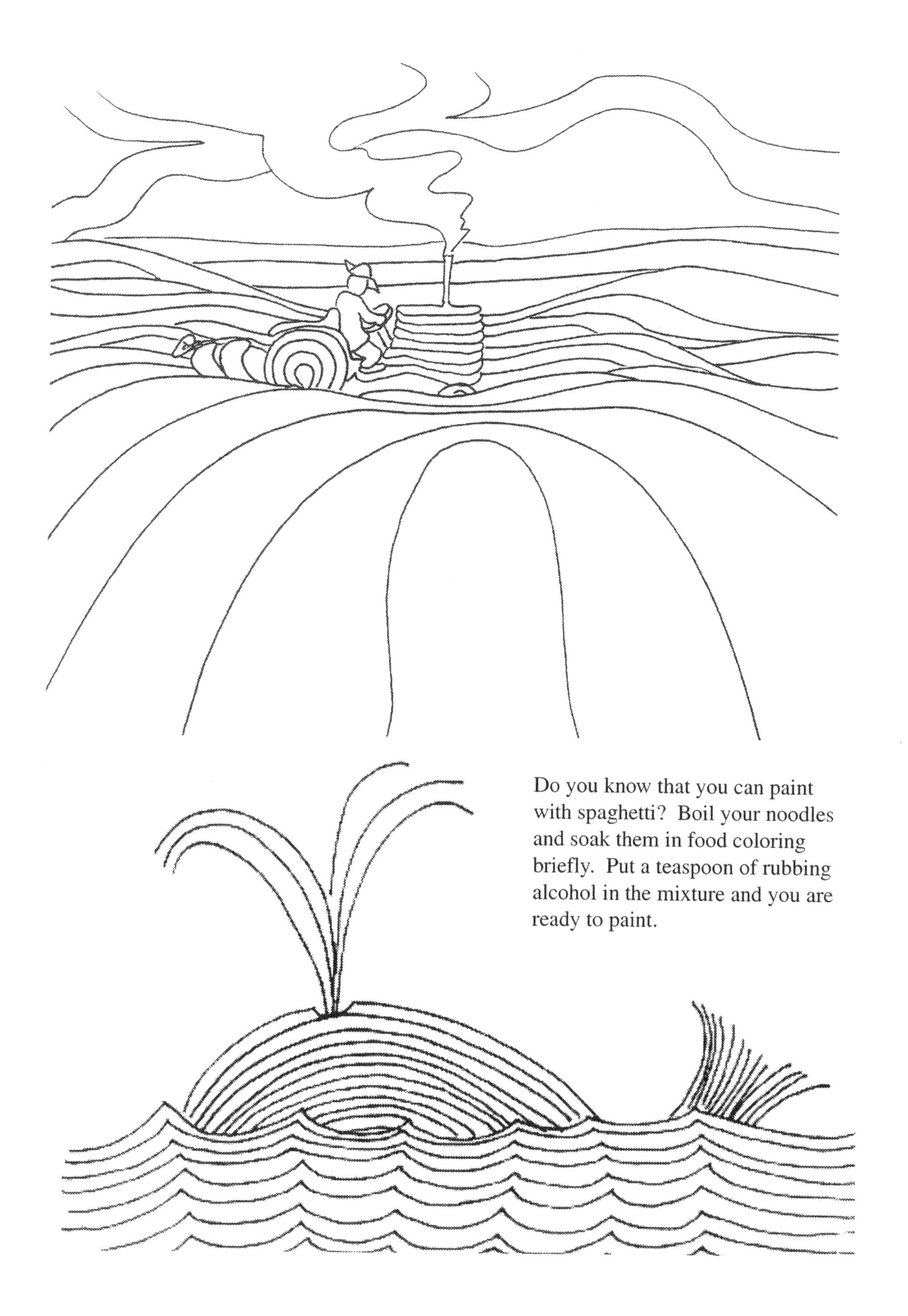

Do you know that you can paint with spaghetti? Boil your noodles and soak them in food coloring briefly. Put a teaspoon of rubbing alcohol in the mixture and you are ready to paint.

4
EXPRESSIONS

4

You can learn to make expressions. Here is how to make 4 different expressions on clown faces. Can you make all 4? Can you make the hair look sad or happy? Notice the eyebrows. Can you move your eyebrows?

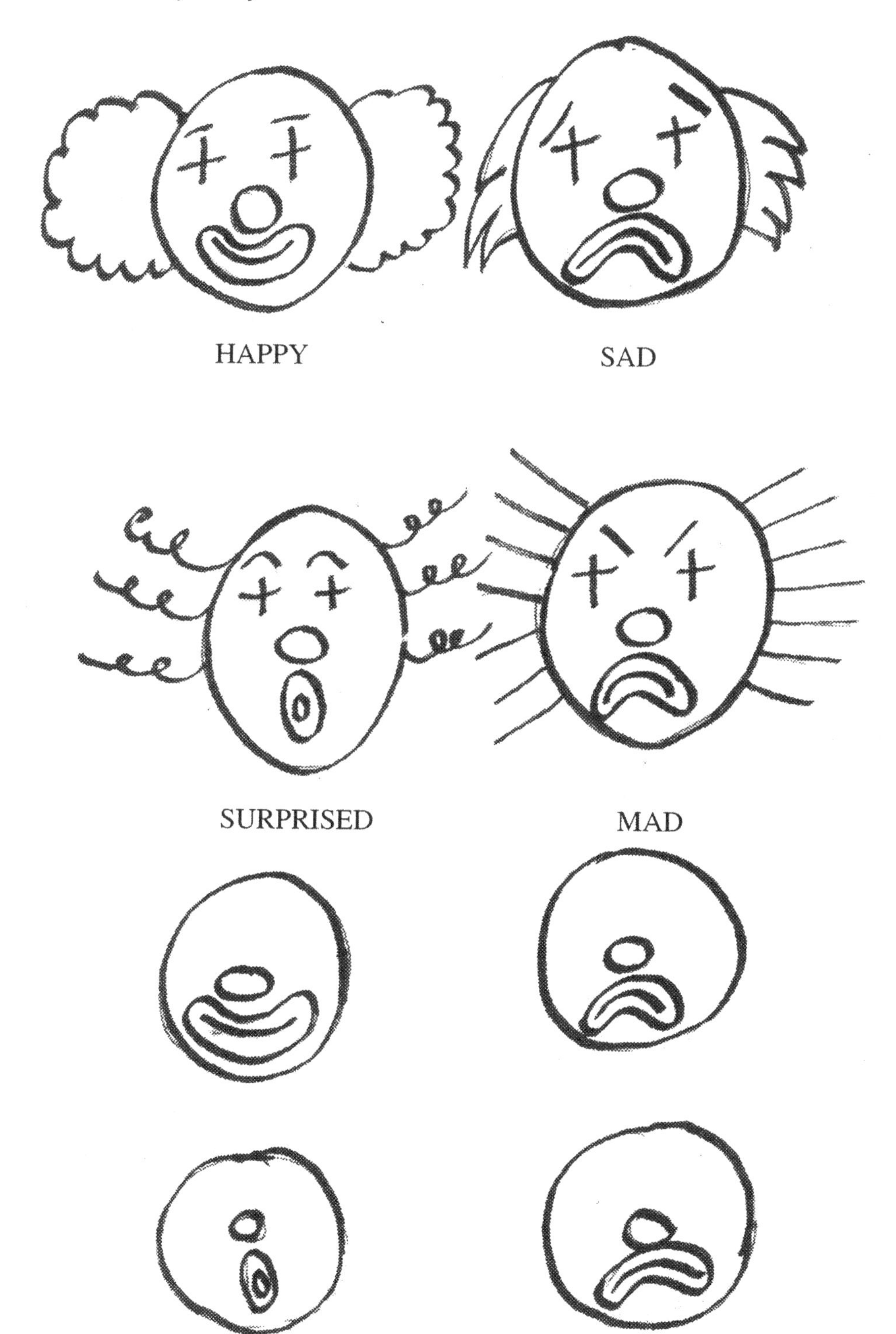

Finish these clowns.

Mt. Rushmore by Gutzon Borglum

How many faces do you see on the previous page? Have you ever seen something blow up? The amazing thing about this great work of art is that 90% of it was carved with dynamite. Do you have a mountain or hill near you? Would you consider sculpting something out of it? Have you ever tried to make faces in the sand or the mud? Borglum had help with this work. He had miners help him. This is **two dimensional art**. It is something that is carved into a surface. If you could go all the way around it, it would be **three dimensional art**. Sometimes you can see things in the clouds. Borglum saw faces in a rock mountain. Can you count the faces? These are four of our presidents. Use these recipes to make clay, or purchase modeling clay from the store and sculpt 4 of your favorite people.

Edible Clay

1 cup smooth peanut butter
1 1/3 cups of powdered milk
3 tablespoons honey
Mix in bowl. You are ready to sculpt and eat!

Sawdust Clay

2 to 4 cups of sawdust
1 cup of wallpaper paste
Mix with water and knead to get clay. Let clay air dry overnight or bake in oven at 350 degrees.

Salt Play Clay

1/2 cup salt
1/2 cup hot water
Mix and bring to boil.
1/4 cup cold water
1/2 cup cornstarch
mix together and add mixture to boiling liquid. Stir until stiff. Knead when cool.

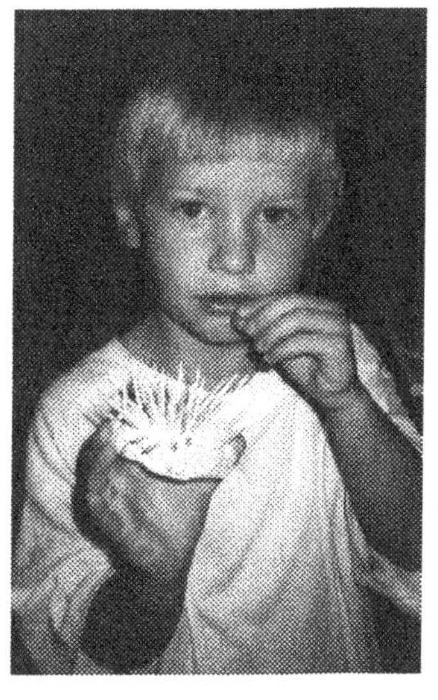

Jeremiah Witek age 4

One of my very favorite sculpting projects to do with little ones is a spiny anteater. This is a monotreme and looks something like a porcupine. Putting toothpicks in the celluclay base is a fine motor skill activity that little ones love. You can purchase celluclay at your local discount store.

More on Borglum

Borglum was not always a sculptor in the west. He lived in Stamford, Connecticut and created many important works. He had a great vision to do the faces of four presidents in the rock. The first plan was to carve sculpture from the needles and granite spurs of the Black Hills. He decided instead that Mt. Rushmore would be the perfect place. According to Borglum's granddaughter, his philosophy on creating was, " *The reason for building any work of art can only be for the purpose of fixing in some durable form a great emotion, or a great idea, of the individual, or the people.*" He did 60 foot high faces of Washington, Jefferson, Theodore Roosevelt, and Lincoln. He used dynamite and a drill. This is called **subtractive** sculpture. It is very difficult. When you make something out of **additive** sculpture, you can add and change it. Subtractive sculpture is different. When you eliminate something, you cannot just put it back on. It took 14 years to finish this great work of art. Can you imagine working on something for even one year?
If you were going to do a sculpture of a mountain with four famous people, who would you choose?

You can practice drawing people. Make the eyebrows on the boy look sad. Make the eyebrows on the girl look mad. Eyebrows are very important!

Have you ever heard the expression, "When pigs fly!" Richard Jeffus did these drawings above of flying pigs. Can you label each pig? One is happy; one sad; one mad, and one surprised.

On the right is a very famous picture by Leonardo da Vinci. It is called *Virgin of the Rocks*. The lady is the mother of baby Jesus. Do you remember which picture Leonardo da Vinci did at the beginning of the book? There are four people in this picture. Can you count the people? Look at the background of the picture. Does it look like you can see far away? Do you think their expression is peaceful?

Virgin of the Rocks
by Leonardo da Vinci

For a large color picture of *Virgin of the Rocks* go to: <http://sunsite.dk/cgfa/vinci/p-vinci14.htm>.

5
SHAPES

You can make many pictures just using these basic shapes. They are made from **horizontal, diagonal** and **vertical** lines...and circular movement of your pencil. Practice these shapes and say the names as you make the shapes. What can you put together out of these shapes? Here is an elephant. Can you name the shapes?

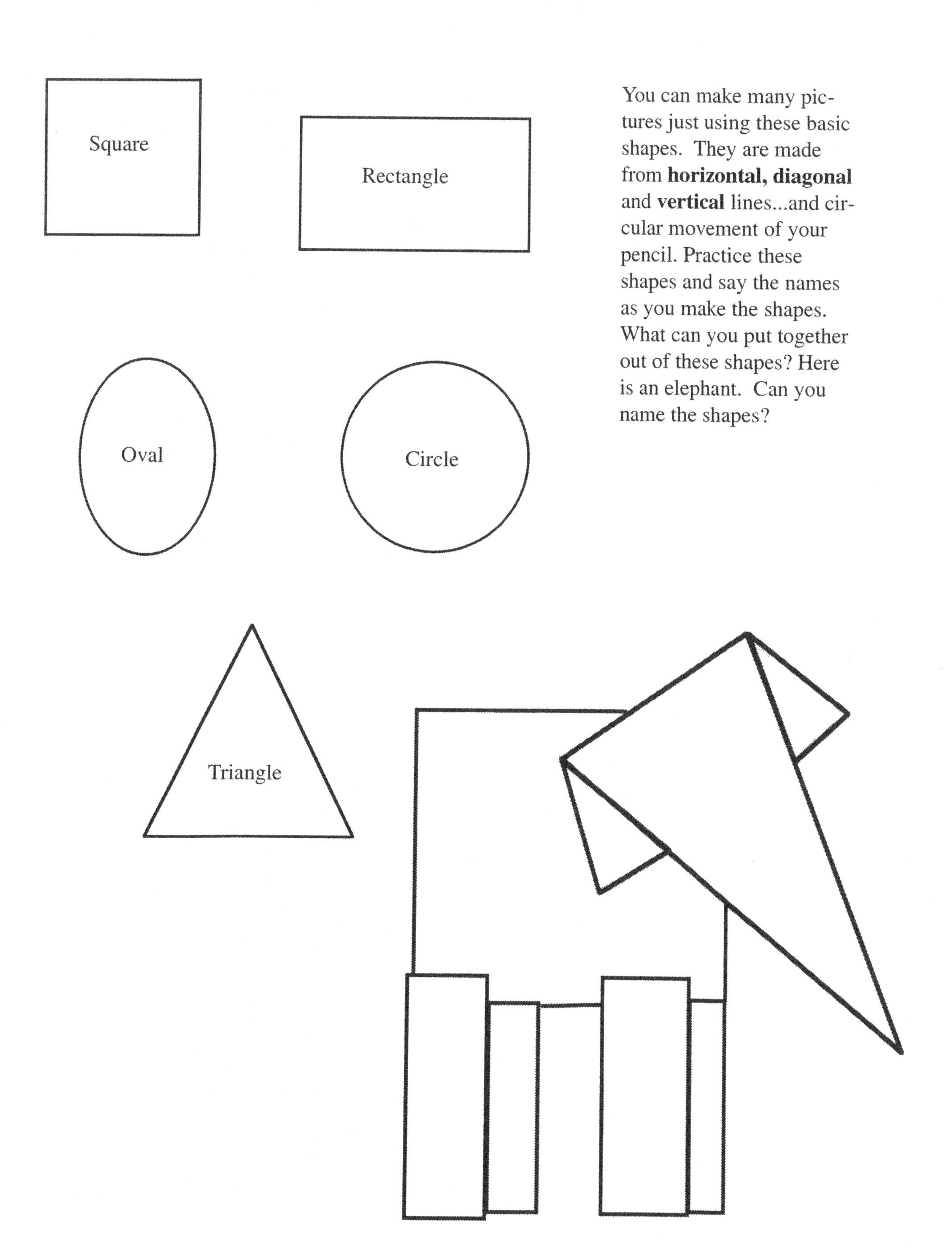

Let's learn to make a tree. There are many different ways to make a tree. Here are just some of them. Can you make a **triangle**? Can you make a **vertical** line? Can you make a **rectangle**? Can you cut and tear paper into the shape of leaves? Then you can make a tree.

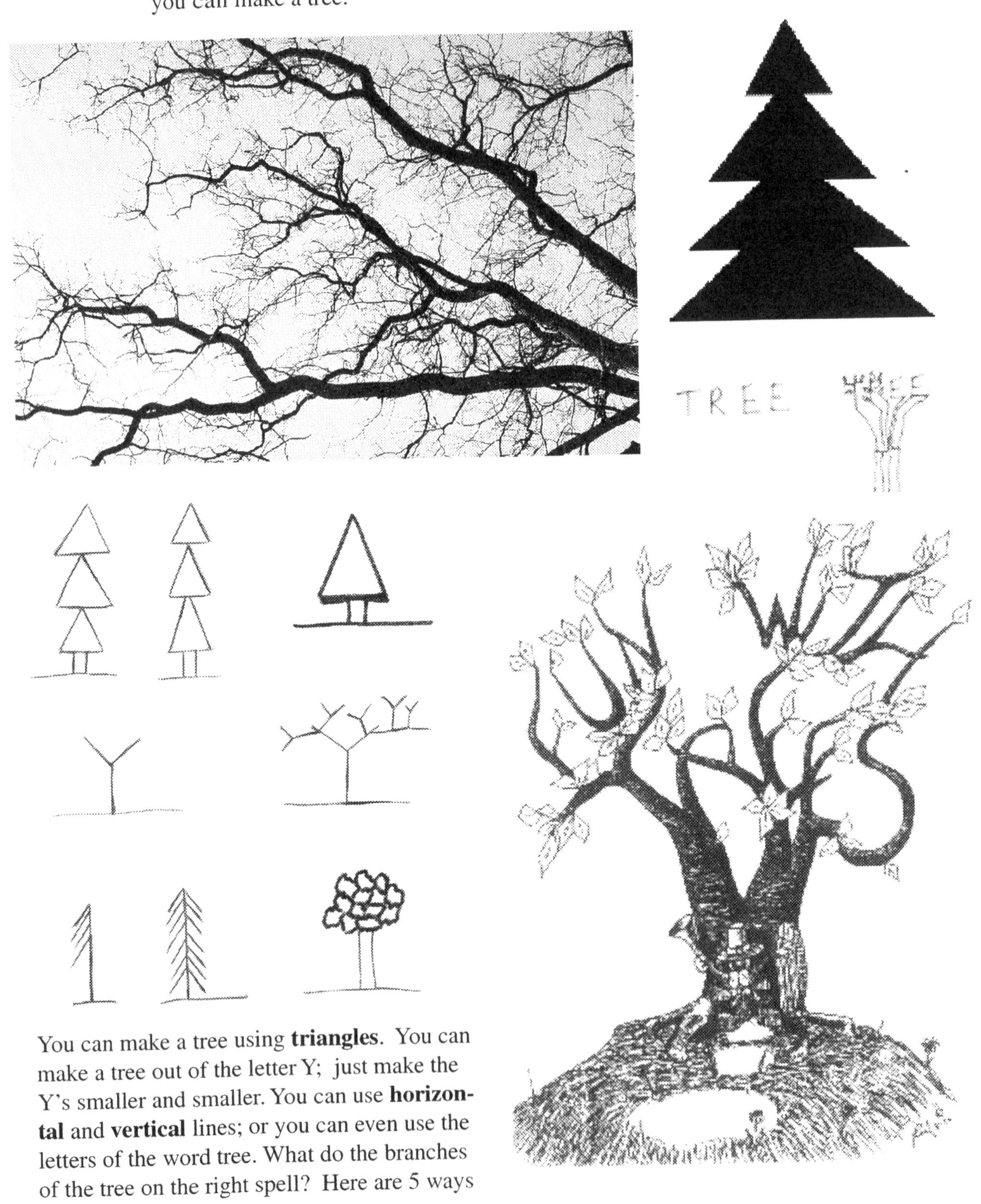

You can make a tree using **triangles**. You can make a tree out of the letter Y; just make the Y's smaller and smaller. You can use **horizontal** and **vertical** lines; or you can even use the letters of the word tree. What do the branches of the tree on the right spell? Here are 5 ways to make a tree.

You can make a sunflower from basic lines and shapes. What might you find on a sunflower?

I always mention the bugs you might find. How many legs would each bug have;how about a spider?

Hannah Batista Age 5 We love it, Hannah!

6
COLOR
WHEEL
COLORS

Color Wheel
Color in the colors of this color wheel.

Can you make a **color wheel** into an owl? Can you make a color wheel into a fish? Use your imagination and turn this color wheel into something special.

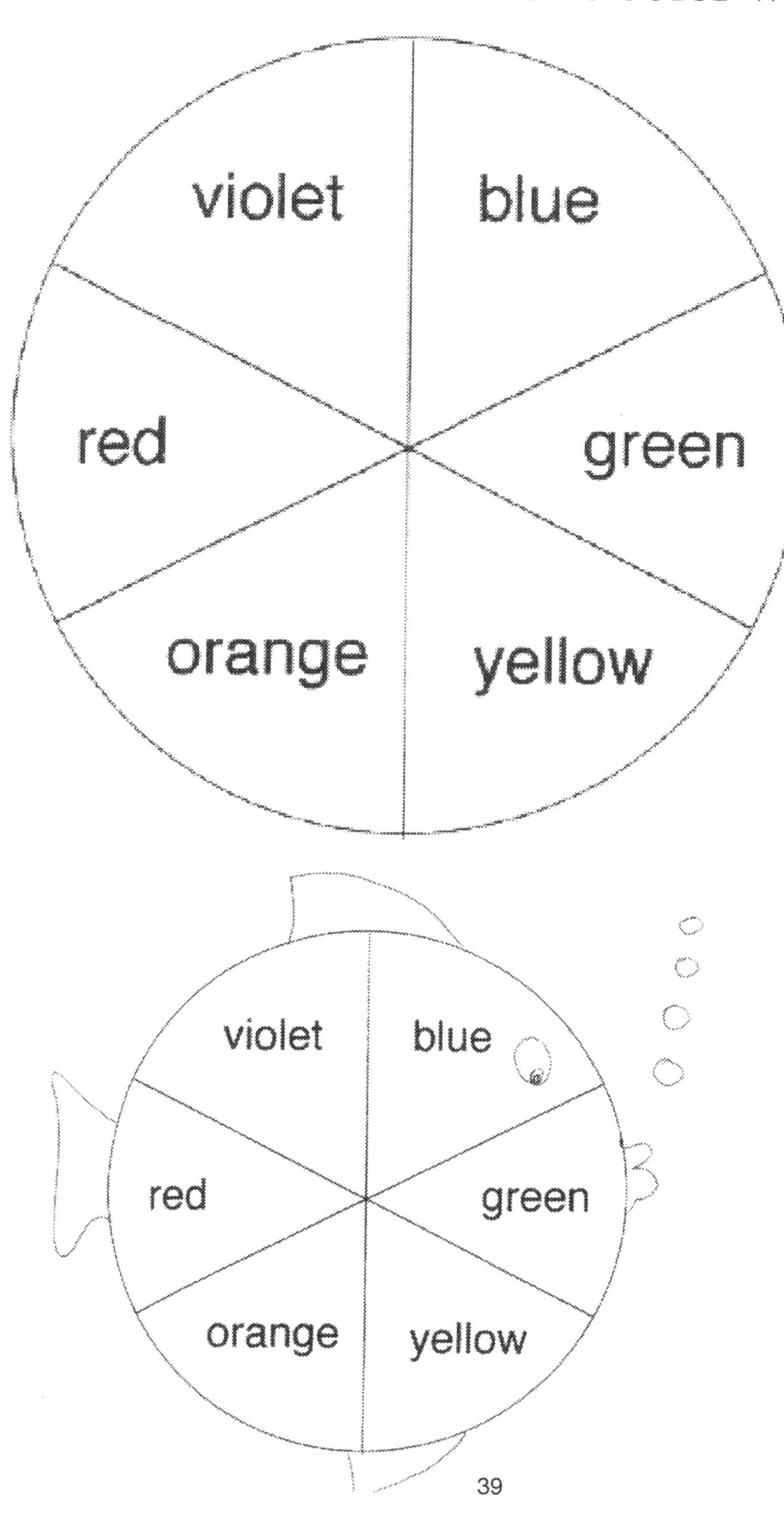

6

There are six colors in the color wheel. There are six colors in a rainbow. Fill in the colors in this color wheel. Fill in the colors in this rainbow. Can you draw a tree with a rainbow over it? Can you put a rainbow on your horse landscape? Can you put a rainbow over your riverboat you made? Can you put a rainbow over your tall ship?

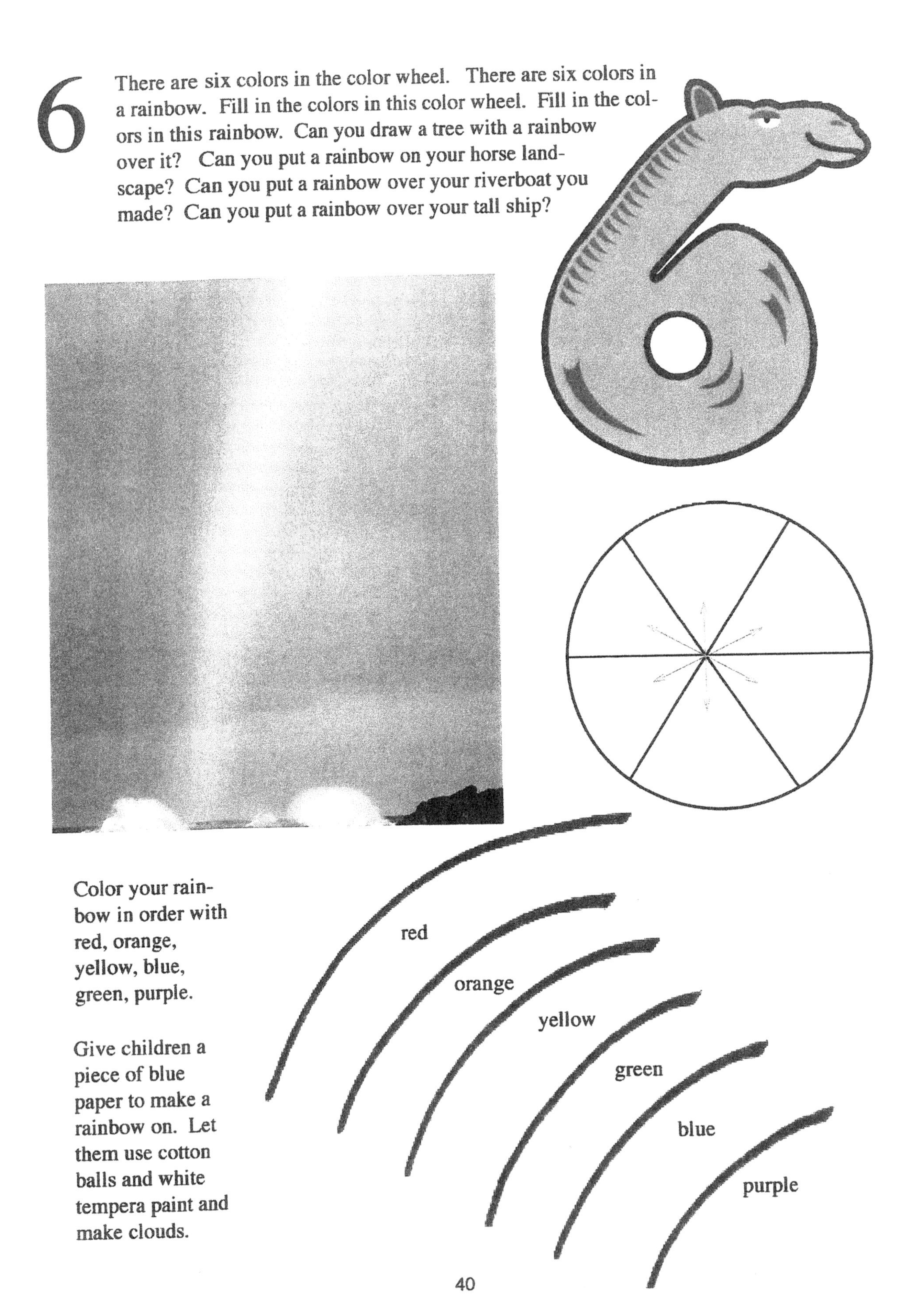

Color your rainbow in order with red, orange, yellow, blue, green, purple.

Give children a piece of blue paper to make a rainbow on. Let them use cotton balls and white tempera paint and make clouds.

You can draw any of these pictures. Instead of coloring them in the usual way, color each one in the colors of the rainbow. You can start with 2 circles, and add triangles and rectangles and have a bear!

How did we get the Teddy Bear? The artist/cartoonist Clifford Berryman did this picture and a toymaker was inspired to create a toy bear!

Look on the next page to see how to draw a bear. When you have drawn your bear, dress him up!

Variety- different forms of the same thing. Each bear is still a bear, but is dressed differently.

For a terrific story of how the Teddy Bear got started go to <http://www.kytales.com/cberr/cberr.html>. You will find out all about Clifford Berryman.

A teddy bear is made from basic shapes. Can you make one?

Color the bear on the right in the shades of the color wheel. Start at the top and color the first part red, then orange, then green, then blue, then yellow and then purple.

7
KINDS OF
PATTERNS

7 Preschool/Kindergarten

A hot air balloon can be made by using a circle, and **vertical**, **horizontal** and **diagonal** lines. A **pattern** is a repeated design. When you put dots on something, you have made a pattern. When you put lines on something, you have made a pattern. Things in the **foreground** are larger, things in the **background** are smaller. Some of the balloons look smaller, because they are far away. The ones closer to you look larger. Can you make seven hot air balloons? Put patterns on each one. Can you make each pattern different?

Look at the pattern on the leopard.

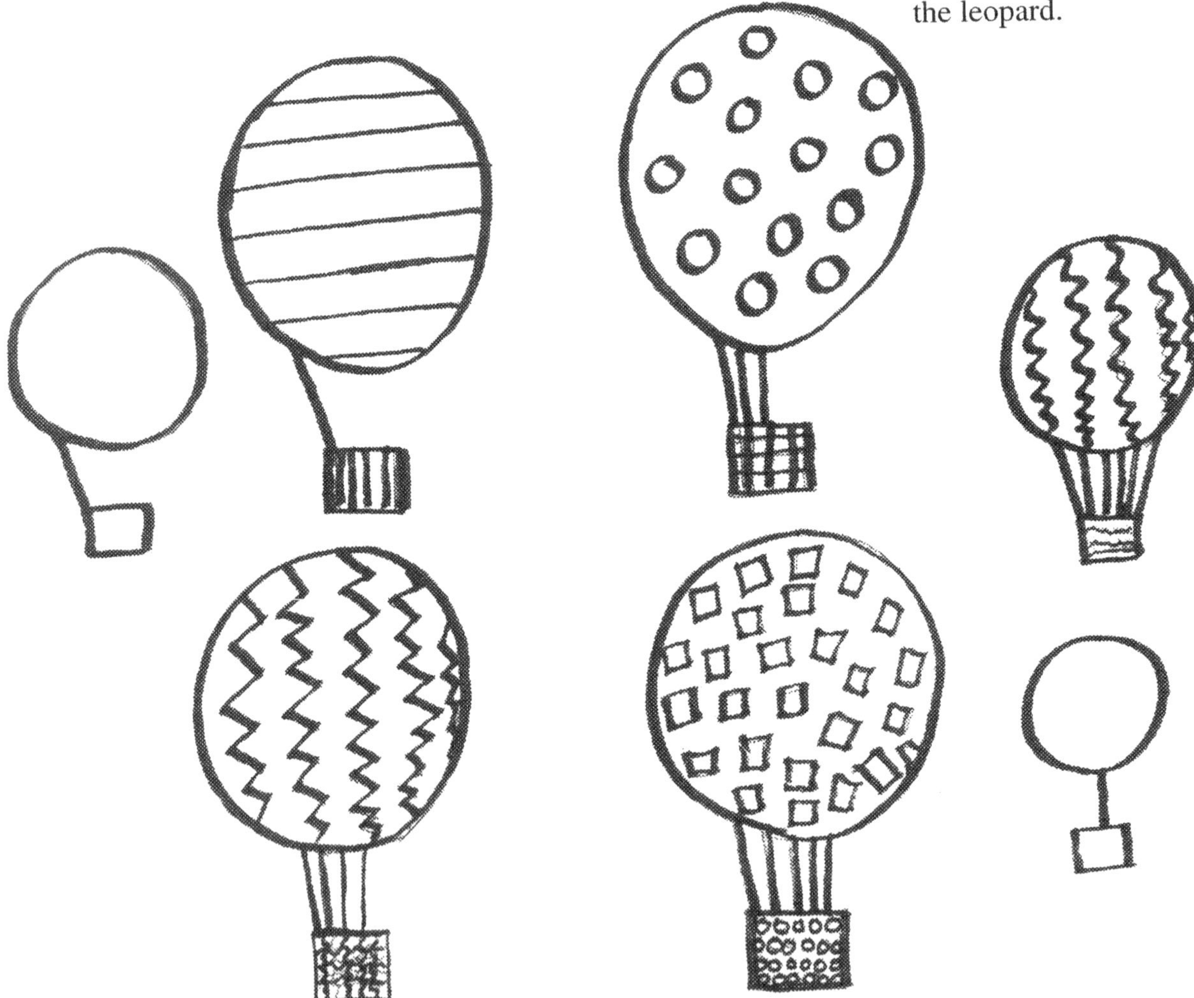

To illustrate **primary colors**, allow the children to make a red hot air balloon with a yellow basket on a blue sky color paper. Tell them the three primary colors are red, yellow and blue. Now let them make patterns on the balloon and basket. A **pattern** is a repeated design.

A **PATTERN** IS A REPEATED DESIGN.

Put a different pattern on each part of the clown and each balloon.

For a wonderful still life by Henri Matisse called "Bouquet of Dahlias and White Book", go to <http://sunsite.dk/cgfa/matisse/p-matisse22.htm>.

A **still life** is a grouping of inanimate objects. A **pattern** is a repeated design.

One of my favorite projects to do with little ones is to make a tablecloth first. I let them make a pattern on their table cloth. We only use the three **primary colors** for the entire picture. We name which fruits and vegetables are red, which are yellow, and which are blue. It is lots of fun to let them think of the fruits and vegetables and let them draw them with you!

THE THREE **PRIMARY COLORS** ARE RED, YELLOW AND BLUE.

Point to the patterns seen on these birds.

8
KINDS
OF BIRDS

8 It is fun to make a bird. I like to put a bird on a fence. Do you remember how to make an owl? Do you remember how to make a tree? Where might you see a bird? You could see a bird on a fence. Draw two fence posts and connect them with horizontal lines. Since this is a barbed wire fence, we are going to put short vertical lines crossing the horizontal ones. In my bird picture, you can count three triangles and two circles. Can you make a bird on a fence? Make eight birds and try to make each a little different. It is important that you show variety.

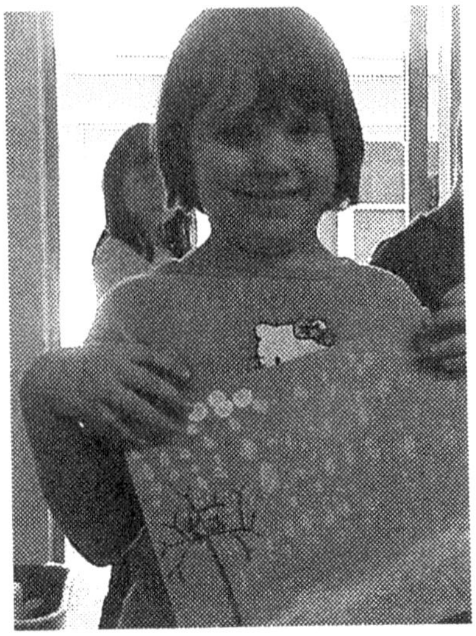

Natalie Joy Dominguez
Age:6

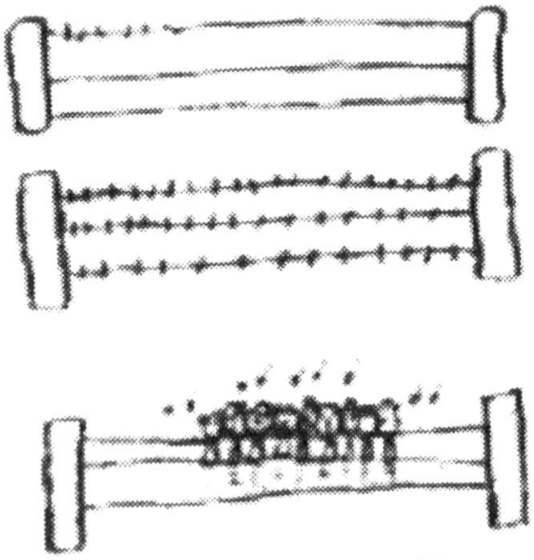

EAGLE

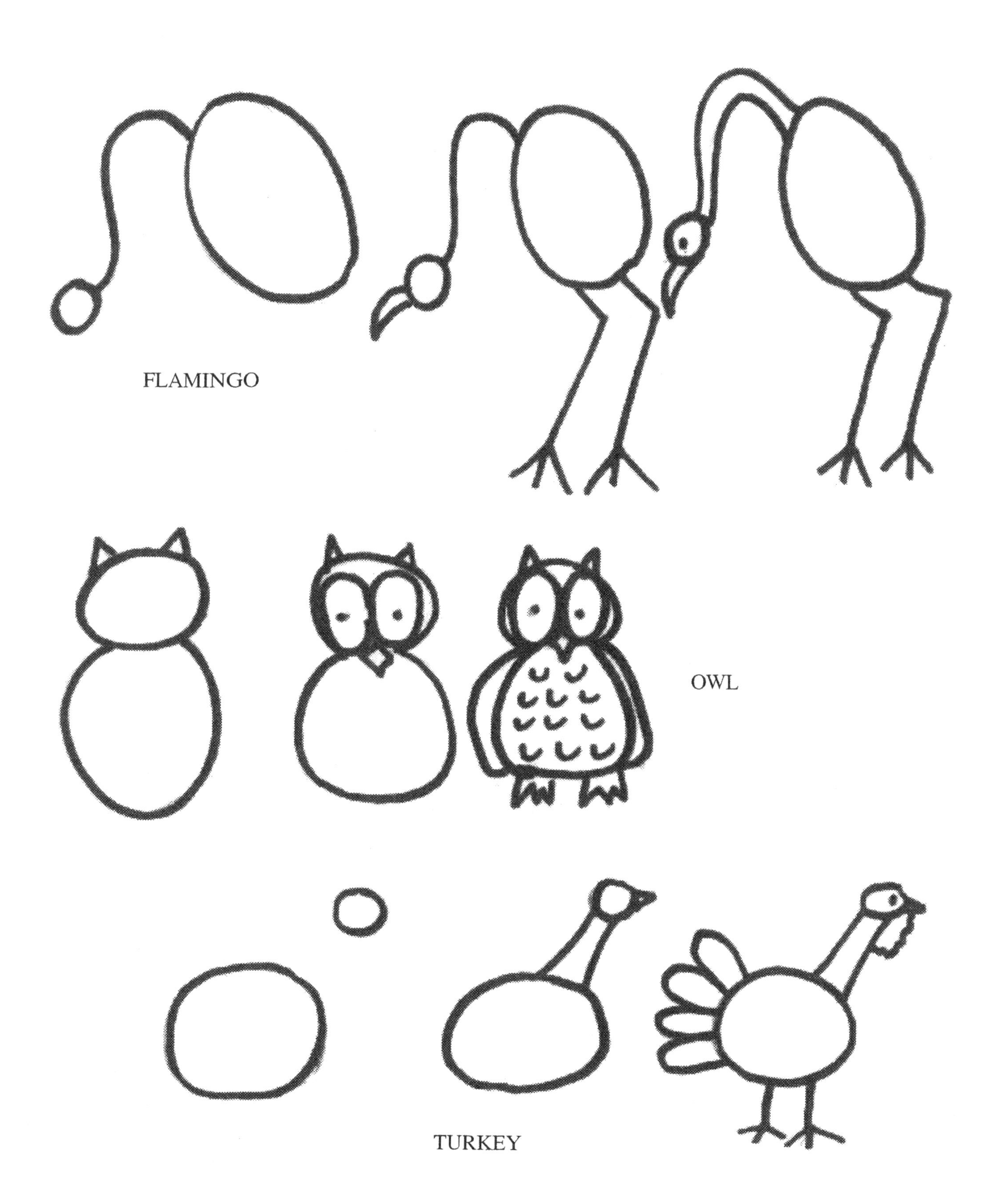
FLAMINGO
OWL
TURKEY

For a wonderful color closeup of an Audubon color picture go to: <http://sunsite.dk/cgfa/a/p-audubon1.htm>.

Have you ever made a mistake in a picture and thought it was ruined? According to Three Hundred Years of American Painting, by Elliot, the great bird artist Audubon did a picture of his young wife in water color. He thought he made a mess of it. He didn't like it. So instead of throwing it away, he put chalk pastel over it and tried to fix it. That remained the way he did his work for all of his life. Maybe you will look at the directions of drawing a bird, and do a picture of birds with your crayons. If you are not satisfied, or even if you are; get your paints and add paint to your bird picture.

American Flamingo engraved by Robert Havell from a picture by John James Audubon

More on Audubon

Audubon was quite a character. Audubon wore buckskins and dressed like a frontiersman. He knew the birds of America better than any person in early American history, so he decided to do a book. He was not able to get it published in America, so he went to England. The people in England really loved him. They loved him because he told people in Europe what life was like in America. Sir Walter Besant told him, "Brave is the exhibition of flowing locks;they flow over the ears and over the coat collars; you can smell the bear's grease across the street; and if these amaranthine locks were to be raised you would see the shiny coating of bear's grease upon the velvet collar below." English publishers Robert Havell and Son agreed to publish his 435 bird pictures in a book. Audubon got 161 patrons in England, Europe and America to give $100.00 each to publish his book. *"No one, I think,* Audubon declared, *paints in my method; I, who have never studied but by piecemeal, form my pictures according to my ways of study. For instance, I am now working on a fox; I take one neatly killed, put him up with wires and when satisfied with the truth of the position, I take my palette and work as rapidly as possible; the same with my birds; if practicable I finish a bird at one sitting--often it is true of fourteen hours--so that I think they are correct, both in detail and composition."*

Kathleen Powell age 5

9
THINGS TO
SHOW SCALE

9

Dinosaurs

Can you make 9 dinosaurs? Richard Jeffus had some people come and ask him to do pictures for their latest book on dinosaurs. They wanted him to illustrate it. Every picture book you have has an artist who did the pictures for you to be delighted in and enjoy!

Drawing dinosaurs with wee little ones needs to be kept simple. I emphasize "C"shapes and lines.

Practice drawing these dinosaurs.

Victoria Johnson Age 7

Learning to Show Scale

Our first drawing to show scale is to draw a tree beside this dinosaur. Look at Victoria's dinosaur. If a tree is the size of a tree at your house, How big is the dinosaur?

I precut brown tree trunks and pass them out to the little ones. I also precut tissue paper squares in shades of green that we scrunch up and glue on the top of our tree.

This dinosaur is made out of circles, rectangles and triangles. You can add the details.

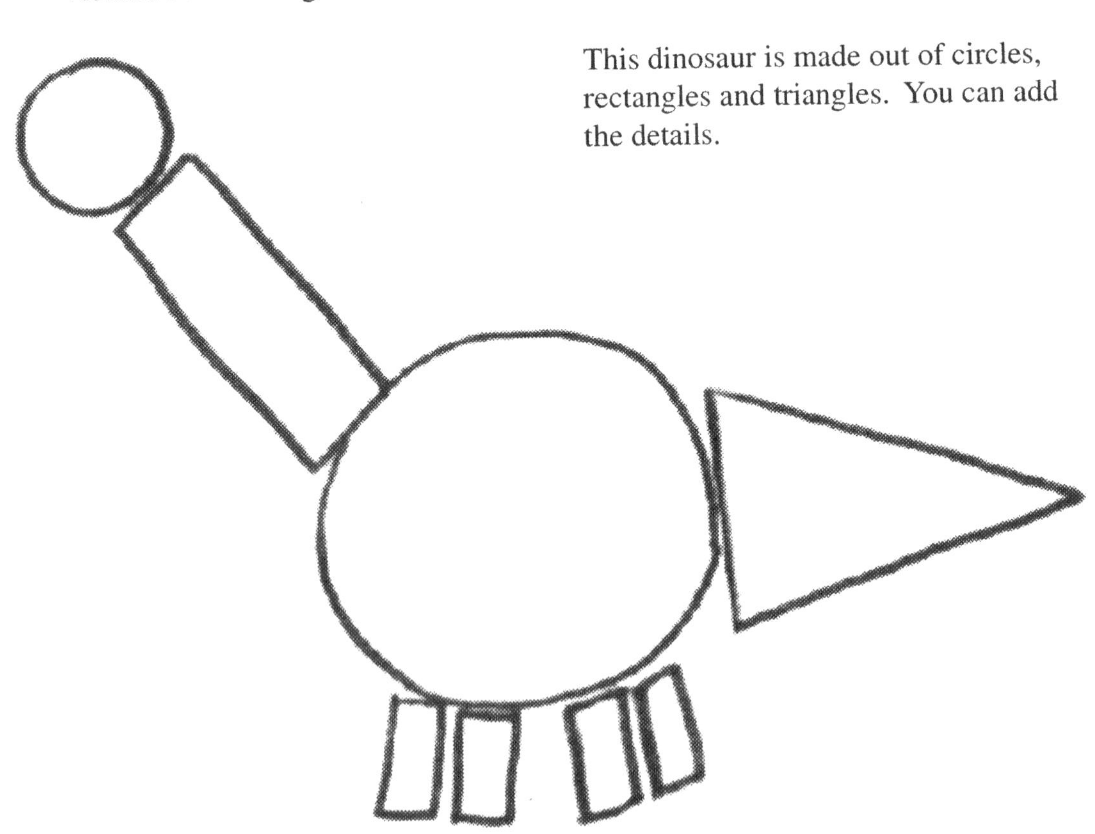

If the rhino in the center is the size of a real rhino, how big are the dinosaurs? Here is a caterpillar below. When you make a caterpillar, you **overlap** one circle over another. This is seen in the above picture when Mr. Jeffus overlaps his dinosaurs. Do you remember your sunflower? You can put a caterpillar climbing up the stem.

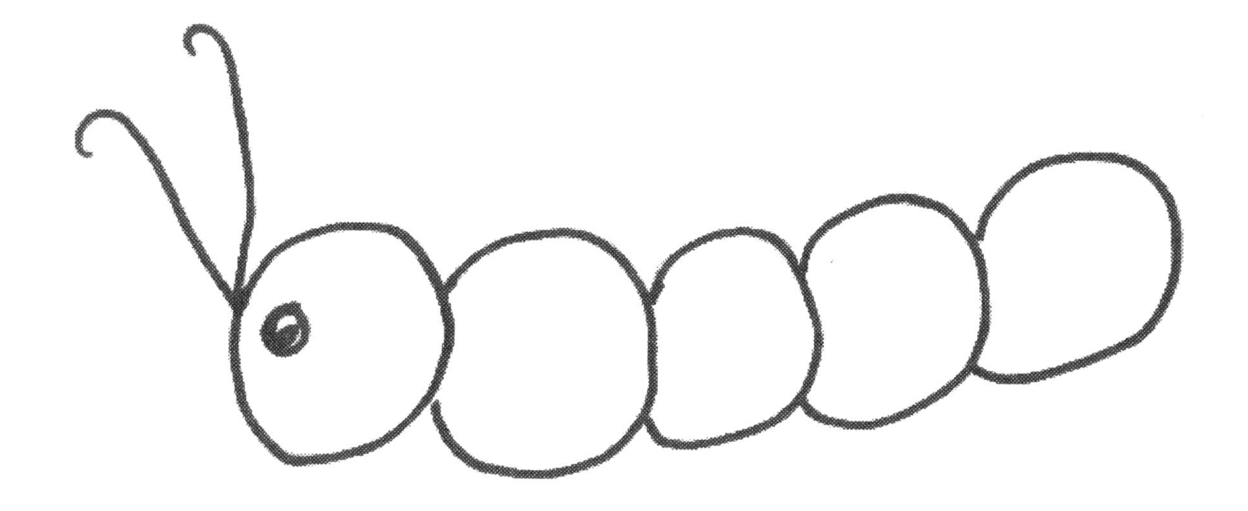

If the viking is the size of a man, how big is the dinosaur?

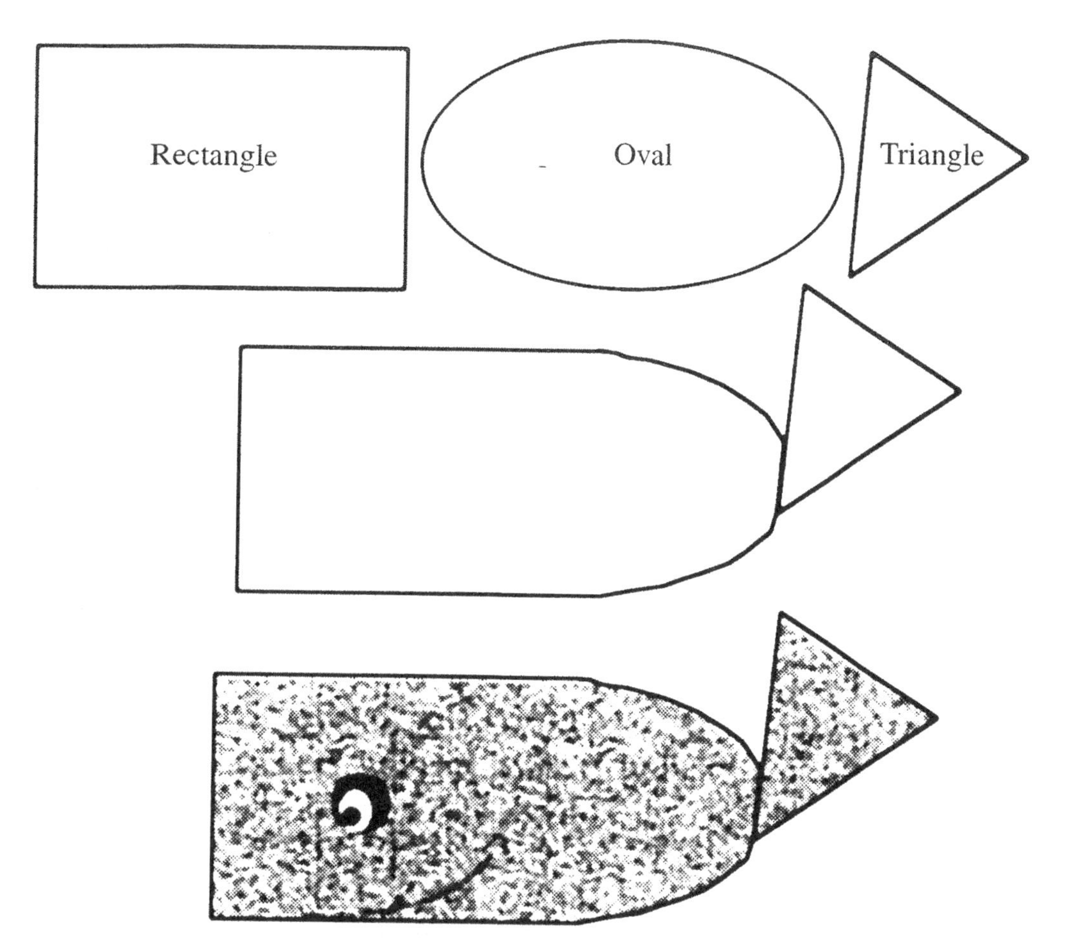

You know how big this whale is by looking at the size of the room and the people. Can you make a whale and then put it beside your dinosaur so we will know what size your dinosaur is?

You learned how to draw a tall ship. How big is this sea monster/dinosaur if the tall ship is the size of a real tall ship? Draw a tall ship and then draw your dinosaur beside it. The tall ship is in the background of the picture. Things in the foreground are closer than things in the background. Things in the foreground are bigger than things in the background. How big do you think this dinosaur is?

You learned how to draw a horse. Can you draw a dinosaur and put a horse beside the dinosaur? How big you make your horse next to your dinosaur will tell us how big your dinosaur is.

Draw a frog beside this dinosaur. How big you make your frog will tell us how big your dinosaur is.

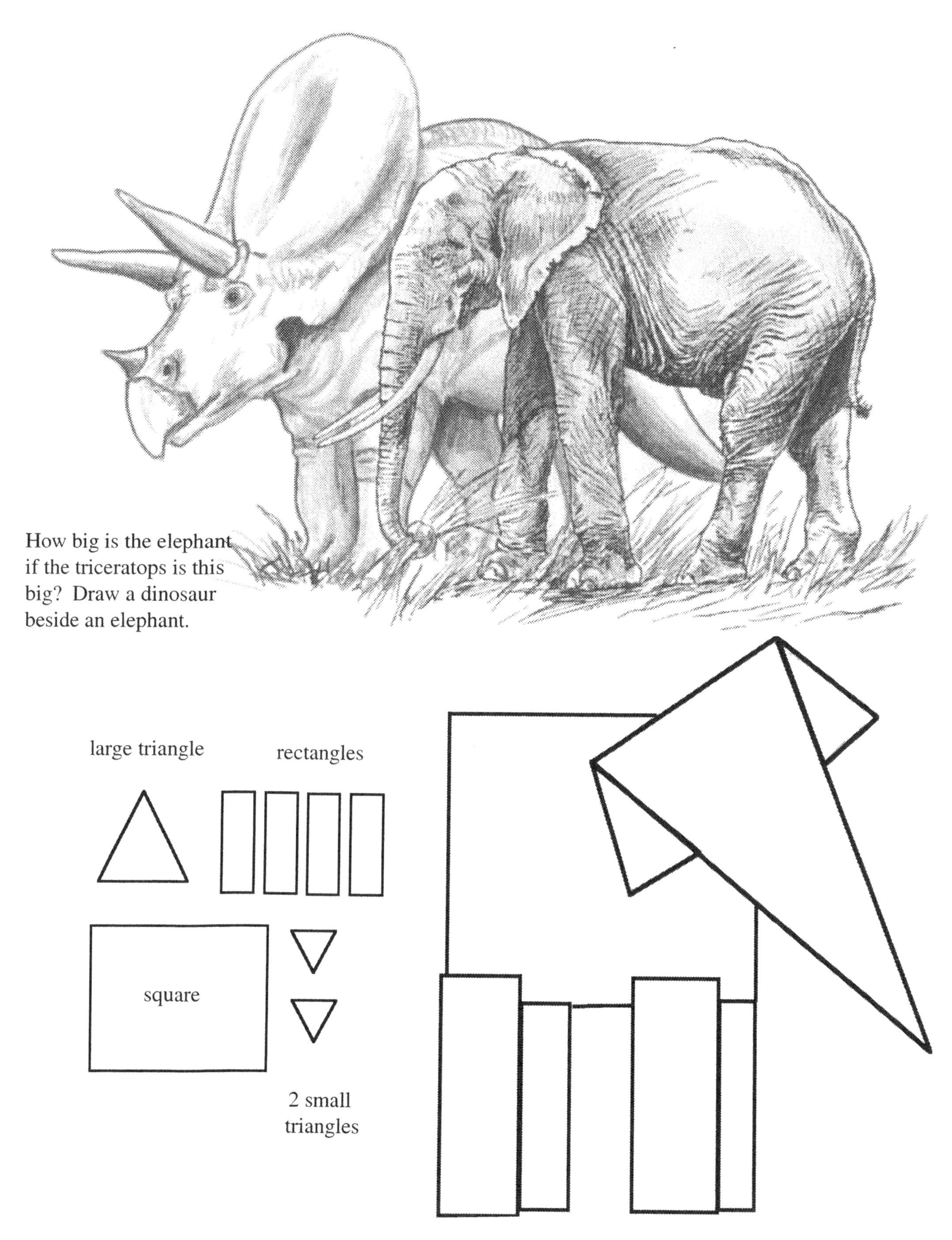

How big is the elephant if the triceratops is this big? Draw a dinosaur beside an elephant.

Draw a dinosaur first, and then draw a girl. How big is the dinosaur if the girl is the size of a normal girl? Use the directions in lesson 4 to draw a girl. Do you see that the girl is holding a baby dinosaur?

Richard Jeffus is an artist who loves dinosaurs. Here are some of his pictures for a book he is illustrating. He loves dinosaurs so that is what he likes to do in art. He draws them, he paints them, and he sculpts them. Many artists choose one subject and spend their life communicating about it. David Plank is a famous bird artist who started drawing birds in the first grade. Now he makes his living painting birds. Nelson and Miller paint beautiful scenes from under the sea. Remington and Russell painted scenes of the early American west. What is something you love to do pictures of?

Can you count the dinosaurs? There are 9 dinosaurs.

Go to the web site below and see a very famous work of art called *St. George and the Dragon* by one of the great artists of the high Italian Renaissance. Look at the beautiful princess. Look at the brave knight. He is killing something that is called a dragon. Some people think that it might be a dinosaur that has since become extinct. Notice the town far in the distance. Notice how the top of the picture is darker at the top of the sky and gets lighter as it goes down. Richard Jeffus did a copy of this painting and substituted the dragon in the original for the raptor dinosaur you see on the left. Could dragons really have been dinosaurs? We think so!

Go to this web site to see a large color representation of this picture: <http://sunsite.dk/cgfa/raphael/p-raphae36.htm>.

Janson's History of Art says that, "The genius of Raphael was a unique power of synthesis that enabled him to merge the qualities of Leonardo and Michelangelo, creating a work that is at once lyric and dramatic, pictorially rich and sculpturally solid." To make it simple, Raphael combined some of the best elements of the other two great masters of the high Italian Renaissance, but died at a very young age. His master work of art, "School of Athens," is considered a perfect example of a high Renaissance work of art.

On the left is a picture from one of the earliest printed books, the *Hortus Sanitatis.* The printing date was between 1475 and 1500. Could that be a dinosaur beside that bear?

10
PLACES
TO LIVE

10

You can make many wonderful things out of rectangles. Can you make a rectangle? If you can, then you can make them vertically (a line that stands up), and you will have a city. You can make them horizontally (a line that lies flat like it is sleeping), and you will have a cabin. You can follow directions and make them both ways and have a castle. Did you ever think of someone who designs buildings as an artist? He is called an **architect** and he is an artist. A person who designs a chair is an artist. A person who designs what you wear is an artist. Let's try to make some places people can live.

TEPEE
IGLOO
TREE HOUSE

RECREATIONAL VEHICLE (RV)

GRASS HUT
HOUSEBOAT

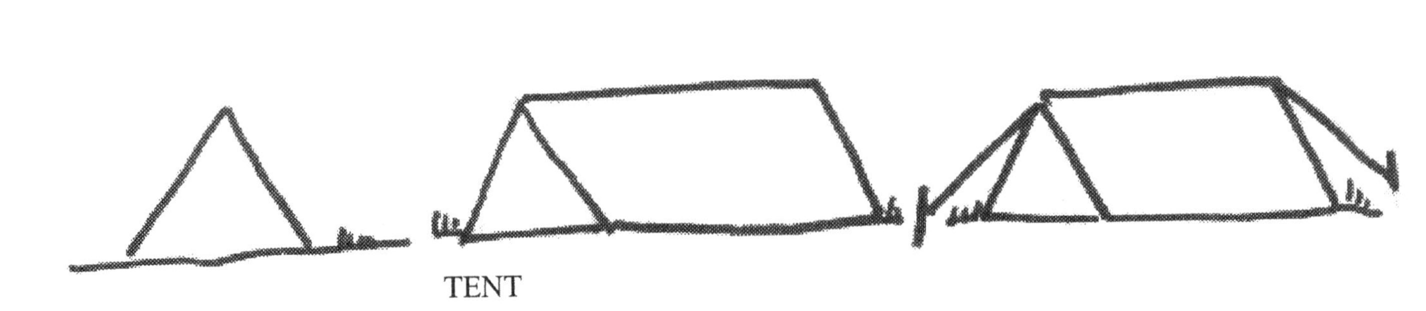
TENT

For a color picture of this beautiful castle and a story of its history go to:
<http://www.germanworld.com/neu.htm>.

A building that is a true architectural wonder is the Sydney Opera House. It is in the country of Australia. It has a beautiful bridge in the background behind the opera house. This would be a difficult structure to draw. Can you try it?

MORE BOOKS FROM VISUAL MANNA

Art Through the Core **series...**

- Teaching American History Through Art
- Teaching Astronomy Through Art
- Teaching English Through Art
- Teaching History Through Art
- Teaching Literature Through Art
- Teaching Math Through Art
- Teaching Science Through Art
- Teaching Social Studies Through Art

Other Books...

- Art Adventures in Narnia
- Art Basics for Children
- Bible Arts & Crafts
- Christian Holiday Arts & Crafts
- Dragons, Dinosaurs, Castles and Knights
- Drawing, Painting and Sculpting Horses
- Expanding Your Horizons Through Words
- Indians In Art
- Master Drawing
- Preschool & Early Elementary Art Basics
- Preschool Bible Lessons
- Visual Manna 1: Complete Art Curriculum
- Visual Manna 2: Advanced Techniques

Books available at Rainbow Resource Center:
www.rainbowresource.com • 888.841.3456

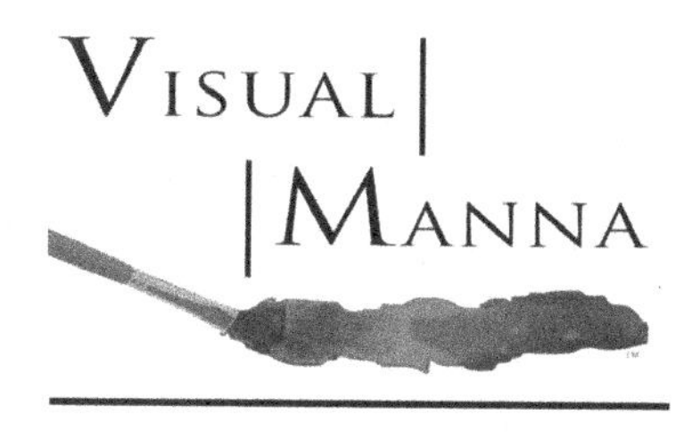

Educating with art since 1992!

A Christian is one whose imagination should fly beyond the stars. Francis Schaeffer

Contact ***visualmanna@gmail.com*** if you are interested in our Intern program. Students learn how to teach art, do murals for ministry, prepare an excellent portfolio, and much more. Go to **visualmanna.com** for information.

Free art lessons are available at **OurHomeschoolForum.com** and books are available at Rainbow Resource Center (**www.rainbowresource.com**). Try all our "Art Through the Core" series and other books as well! Make learning fun for kids!!! Sharon Jeffus teaches Art Intensives in person for the Landry Academy at **landryacademy.com**.

Made in USA - Kendallville, IN
1195319_9781933407975
01.21.2021 1602